GRIEF JOURNAL

Memory Book for Kids

Guided Prompts for Processing Loss & Finding Emotional Healing

THIS JOURNAL BELONGS TO

_____

_____

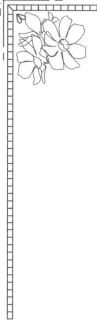

IN MEMORY OF

CONTENTS

INTRODUCTION

Hi there, little one...

My name is Hope and I will try to guide you as best as possible in the journey you are about to embark on. I know you are going through a tough time right now, some time ago I was there too. Because of that, I understand that the loss of someone or something you hold dear is very hard, but I promise that everything will be fine in the end.

I am very glad that somebody thought to give you this book. That person loves you very much and wants to take care of you in the best way possible. This journal was specially designed to help you in these moments. You can think of it as a safe space, where you can give vent to all the emotions that try you. Nothing bad can happen here.

I am sure that the feelings you have now are complicated. Sadness, anger, confusion, fear...one or all may be present. It's normal to feel this way, you just suffered a loss and now you have a whole series of new feelings to explore. It is absolutely OK to be upset.

I don't want you to feel obligated to complete these pages in a certain order or within a certain time frame. Just do what you feel like doing when you feel like doing it, without the pressure of time.

You should be very proud of yourself, expressing your feelings of grief is not an easy thing at all, but I know you can do it. And just remember: when someone you love becomes a memory, the memory becomes a treasure.

Whenever you feel ready, let's start our journey.

HOW TO USE THIS JOURNAL

This workbook includes several activities designed to help you understand the grieving process. By filling each page feel free to express yourself however you want. Go on! You've got this!

The journal is structured as follows:
- <u>Pages that will explain exactly how grief works</u>. By reading these pages, you will understand that everything you feel is normal.
- <u>Guided prompts to help you better process your loss.</u>
- <u>Lots of writing and drawing activities so you can explore all your emotions.</u>
   Please note that a blank page is left after each drawing activity to avoid printing on the other side. Also, the drawing pages will be indicated by the following symbol:

- <u>Unique exercises which are designed to calm you down when your feelings run wild.</u>

Remember that this journal is your safe space and that you can go through it at your own pace. There is no time pressure or order to be followed.

ALL ABOUT ME

This is a picture of me!

My name is _____

I am from _____

I am_____ years old.

I'm in grade_____ at

_____(school).

In my free time I like to:

_____

On weekends I usually:

_____

Someday I want:

_____

At school I like:

_____

My favorite food(s) is/are

_____

My favorite movie is

_____

My bestfriend is

_____

I feel good when

_____

"You may have lost things, persons in your life. But you can capture them in your memories forever."

~ Anonymous

MY MEMORIES OF

_____

Stir positive memories about your loved one. Answer this
simple questions and color it as you wish!

Something they always
said to me:

They loved this COLOR

My favorite thing to do
with them was:

They were always proud
of me because:

I loved about them
that:

They were the best at:

When I want to
remember them I can:

When I feel sad I can
talk to:

"If there ever comes a day where we can't be together, keep me in your heart. I'll stay there forever."

~ A.A. Milne, Winnie the Pooh

WHAT IS GRIEF

Grief is a strong, sometimes overwhelming emotion for people and it appears when they lose someone or something they love. It is the natural reaction to loss and it can affect us in different ways.

This emotion can occur when we encounter different types of loss like the death of someone close to us, loss of a friendship, a breakup, or a pet dying.

We can experience different stages of grief. These phases can come in any order and last for different amount of time.

We can have all sorts of feelings during the process of grieving: sadness, anger, anxiety, shock, or loneliness. It's ok to feel them all!

In order to start feeling better, it is important to find healthy ways of coping with your emotions.

It is essential to remember that grieving has no time limit. You can take all the time you need. It might be helpful to talk to someone about what are you going through.

THE FIVE STAGES OF GRIEF

Hi buddy! How are you hanging in there?

Everyone reacts differently when faced with the death of someone they loved. However, grieving is natural when a person has left our life.

Grief is universal, but also very personal. You may cry, become angry, withdraw, or feel empty. None of these things are unusual or wrong. What is important to know is that you are not alone. Everyone grieves differently, but there are some commonalities in the stages and the order of feelings experienced during grief.

These commonalities are called the five stages of grief:

1. Denial
2. Anger
3. Bargaining
4. Depression
5. Acceptance

How you face every one of these phases is ultimately a personal one. You are dealing with a lot of emotions. But rest assured, you are supported during the entire process.

Denial

You find it really hard to believe that the person you love is gone.
"I can't believe this is happening."

Anger

You may feel angry towards that person or other people.
"This is unfair! It's all your fault!"

Bargaining

You ask yourself if there is something you can do to make this person return.
"Could I have done something to stop this from happening?"

Depression

You are sad because you understand that he/she is gone and won't return.
"I feel so empty inside. I'll never feel better."

Acceptance

You understand that he/she is gone, but you try to get things back to normal the best that you can.
"It is OK to feel sad sometimes and I'm not alone!"

♡ WHAT DO I FEEL? ♡

Sadness, suffering, and mourning are the natural response to an important loss. Any loss can cause a feeling of bitterness.

It is normal to feel depressed, guilty, anxious, or angry at the person who has died, or at someone else entirely. It is your way of coping, but it is important to know that by expressing whatever emotions you are feeling things will start to get better.

Some days you will feel happy or surprised, and your moods will oscillate from one emotion to another very quickly. Just remember, it's okay for this to happen.

This diary was designed to help you understand yourself better, to understand your thoughts and the things you feel.

You will see that little by little you will be able to incorporate your loved one into your life. Do not forget that the purpose of the grief is not to forget this person, but only to get used to the lack of their presence.

You are awesome! You've got this!

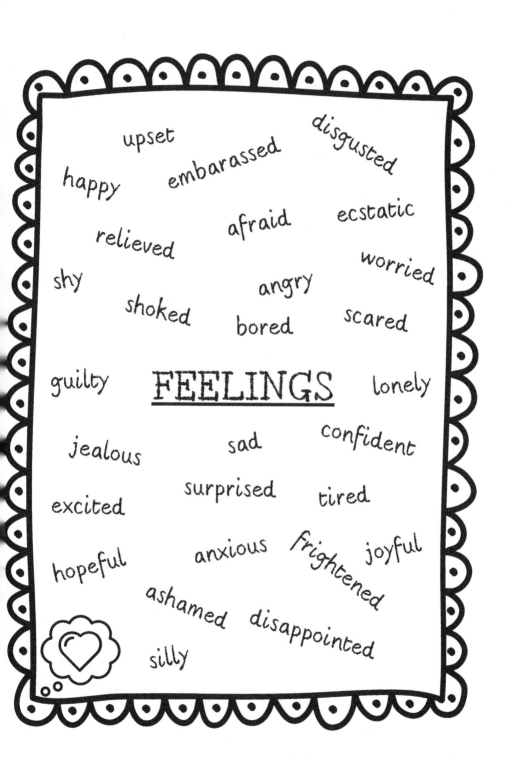

EXPRESSING MY FEELINGS

Circle the feeling or feelings you are experiencing.

ANGRY

SAD

EXCITED

CONFUSED SHOKED

GUILTY

HAPPY

 AFRAID

If what you feel is not found above, don't worry, you can experience a wide range of emotions at certain moments. Just describe what are you feeling the most:

SAY THIS!!!

When you feel sad there are certain things other people can say to make you feel better. There are also some things that can make it worse. When you get sad, what do you need to hear? What don't you want to hear?

SAY THIS

DON'T
SAY THIS

MY TANGLED BALL OF GRIEF

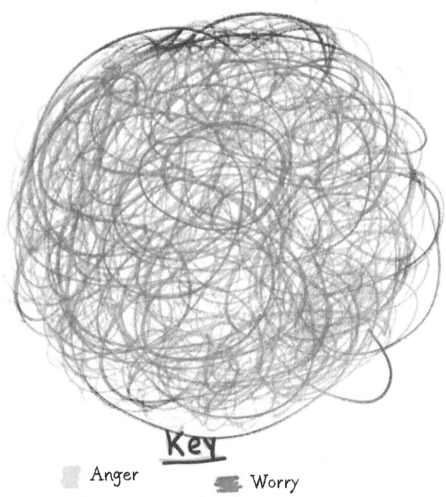

Key

- Anger
- Shock
- Sadness
- Guilt
- Worry
- Emptiness
- Loneliness
- Frustration

Now it's your turn! Create your own tangled ball and express what you feel inside. Please remember that this is a space and you and you can let yourself be simply YOU.

Grab your favorite markers, crayons, or colored pencils, and get started. Choose different colors to represent each different feeling and create your own key.

 You are not judged! You are safe! You are loved!

MY GRIEF PLAN

Make a plan with ways of coping with your feelings of loss and grief. Draw or write down whatever will make you feel better.

When I feel sad, I can do these things to cope:

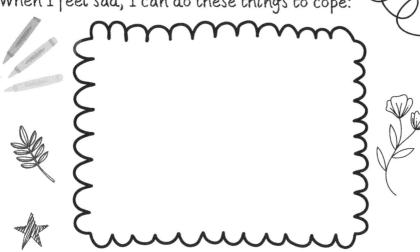

I can talk with these persons to feel better:

I can have these thoughts:

I plan to take care of myself like this:

GRIEF AND MY BODY

Grief can affect many parts of the body. This activity will help you to process your feelings and understand how they feel all over the body. Color the reaction that you are experiencing.

Feeling more or less hungry than usual

Headaches

Hard to concentrate

Trouble sleeping

Crying a lot

Dry mouth

Chest pain

Tense shoulders

Empty feelings in stomach

Slow thinking, speaking, or moving

Body aches

Sweaty palms

Body feels weak and tired

Legs feel weak

Tingling fingers or toes

WHAT I NEED

Draw or write down what it is that you need from every group of people during your grieving process. What can they do to help you the most?

What I need from my family...

What I need from my friends...

What I need from my others...

MY HAPPY PLACE

A happy place is a place where you feel relaxed and safe. It's not necessarily somewhere you have been, it can be an imaginary place. What is important is for you to feel happy there. So, from now on, whenever you are experiencing sadness, anger, or anxiety, just close your eyes and imagine yourself there.

Try to imagine this happy place as vivid and real as you can, so it will be easier for you to calm down when you visit it. Now go on and draw it!

A SPECIAL TIME WITH YOU

It is good to remember special people after they are no longer with us. By doing this we are honoring those persons and we feel closer to them.

Draw or write about a special time you had with your special someone.

Answer the following questions to share more about your memory.

What is happening in this picture?

_____

_____

_____

_____

_____

When did it happen?

_____

_____

_____

_____

Why do you treasure this memory?

_____

_____

_____

_____

What feelings are you experiencing when you think about this memory?

_____

_____

_____

_____

Would you change anything about it?

_____

_____

_____

_____

Write about other memories you have shared with this person.

_____

_____

_____

_____

memories

DRAW THE FEELING

Identify your emotions. Draw a picture or write about when you feel each of them.

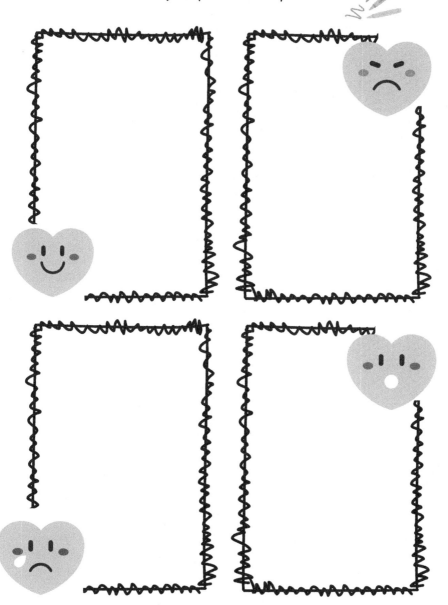

WORRY JAR

A worry jar is a useful tool that can help you express your worries and anxious thoughts. What are some things that make you feel worried? Write/draw them in the jar below.

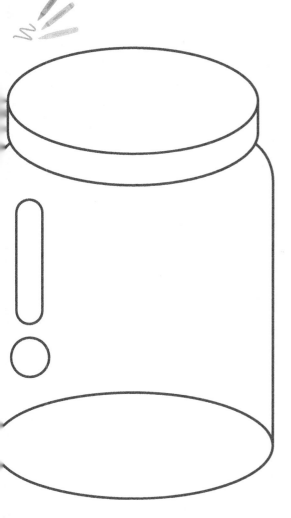

Think of a special time each day when you will open your worry jar and read your worries. You can do this with someone you trust.

What time will you open your worry jar?

Who is going to be with you?

WHO HELPS ME!

Sometimes it is hard to see, but you are loved and supported by so many people. Think about them and write down their name or draw something that represents them.

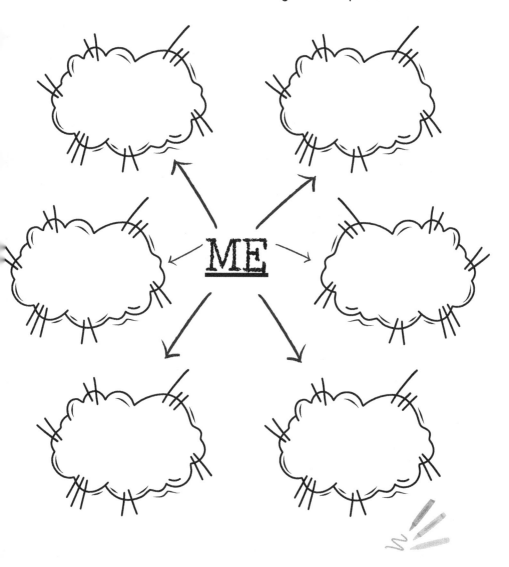

IF FEELINGS COULD TALK OR ACT ♡ ♡

Take a few minutes and imagine what would your feelings tell you if they could talk. What would they tell you to do?

SADNESS would tell me to _____

HAPPINESS would tell me to_____

LONELINESS would tell me to_____

HOPE would tell me to_____

SHAME would tell me to_____

GRATITUDE would tell me to_____

ANGER would tell me to_____

LOVE would tell me to _____

ANXIETY would tell me to _____

INSPIRATION would tell me to _____

IN MY HOUSE, I FEEL....

When we are at home we are the truest version of ourselves. Home is the place where our feelings can be expressed as they are. How do you feel at home?

safe

happy

bored

loved   creative

lonely

confused

accepted

peaceful

angry

understood

?

sad

joyful

scared

guilty

comfortable

★ MY FAMILY ★

Family is always with us regardless of what happens.
They support and love us and expect nothing in return.
Draw a picture to represent your family.

≡♡≡ MY HEART MAP ≡♡≡

Color each space with a color that feels like a specific
emotion, place, or thing that reminds you of your loved one.
Just open your heart. The storm will pass.

You are gonna be OKAY!

JOY JAR

Think about all the things that make you feel happy. Put them in this jar so you can go through them when you're feeling down. Write down or draw, whatever you choose is perfect.

today I CHOOSE joy

THE POWER OF GRATITUDE

During the process of grieving, it can be helpful to remember all the awesome persons and things we have in our lives. Make a list of everything you are grateful for, it will immediately lighten up your mood.

Being thankful is always a good idea!

- [ ] ....
- [ ] ....
- [ ] ....
- [ ] ....
- [ ] ....
- [ ] ....
- [ ] ....

Who were the last 5 people you said "Thank You" to?
Why did you say it?

_____

_____

_____

_____

What were the last three nice things done for you by others?

_____

_____

_____

When you think of grateful or gratitude, what does that mean to you?

_____

_____

_____

If you wanted to show someone you are grateful for
their kindness, how would you show them?

Do you think it takes courage or different life skills to
show gratitude and be thankful?

Name one of your best friends, and describe what
makes them special to you.

What place have you traveled to that you are most grateful for?

_____

_____

_____

_____

What's the most delicious thing you've eaten this week?

_____

_____

_____

_____

Who's someone who always listens when you talk?

_____

_____

_____

_____

UNIQUE ME

Sometimes we are so overwhelmed by the things that surround us that we forget how unique and beautiful we are. You have so many things to be proud of. So many qualities. Share some by coloring and filling every ray of the rainbow.

I AM UNIQUE

Be Kind to Yourself

STAY POSITIVE

Sometimes it is hard to think positively when we are filled with all kinds of feelings. It is important to remember that you don't have to be so hard on yourself. One simple exercise to improve your mood when such things happen is to simply speak kindly to yourself.

I AM ENOUGH

I BELIEVE IN MYSELF

I AM LOVED

I MAKE PEOPLE SMILE

IT'S OK TO MAKE MISTAKES

I TAKE CARE OF MYSELF

I AM BEAUTIFUL

I CAN DO HARD THINGS

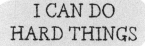

TODAY IS MY DAY

DAY BY DAY

What was the best thing that happened to you today?

_____

_____

_____

_____

What will you do tomorrow that you did not do today?

_____

_____

_____

_____

Did you learn something new today? What was it?

_____

_____

_____

_____

What made you laugh today?

What made you really proud today?

What matters the most to you?

What does being calm look like and mean to you?

What do you feel positive about right now?

What do you love most about yourself?

What is the best gift you have ever given? Why
was it so special?

_____

_____

_____

_____

_____

If you could invent something that would make life
easier for people, what would you invent?

_____

_____

_____

_____

_____

If you could make one rule that everyone in the world
had to follow, what rule would you make? Why?

_____

_____

_____

_____

Did you do anything that was challenging? How did it make you feel?

_____

_____

_____

_____

_____

Which morning routine do you like the most?

_____

_____

_____

_____

_____

If you can change something about your morning routine what would it be? Why do you not like that routine?

_____

_____

_____

_____

What was the funniest thing that happened today?

Did you find yourself in any tricky situations today?
How did you deal with it?

What's the funniest joke that one of your friends has told you?

Tell of a time when you chose to be patient, rather than become angry. What was the outcome? Was it good or bad, and why?

Do you think it is important to manage your emotions and feelings? How could you possibly help others to understand how to manage emotions and feelings?

 MY SUPERPOWER

Let's say you are a superhero with an awesome superpower. What would your really cool superpower be? What would your name be? Draw yourself as the amazing superhero you are in the following box.

BLESSED MORNING

Start every morning with this small exercise. How do you feel after doing it?

5	Slowly take five deep breaths
4	Make a list of four things you see around you
3	Make a list of three things you are grateful for
2	Say two positive things to yourself
1	Say one thing you are looking forward to today.

SELF-CARE CHECKLIST

- [ ] eat 3 meals a day
- [ ] 7+ hours of sleep
- [ ] get fresh air
- [ ] make your bed
- [ ] ask for a hug
- [ ] write in your journal
- [ ] spend time with friends
- [ ] read a book
- [ ] try something new
- [ ] brush your teeth
- [ ] spend time with family
- [ ] do some exercises

STAR BREATHING

Sometimes we can feel overwhelmed because we experience too many feelings at once. Whenever this happens, just do the following exercise. It will help you calm your emotions immediately.

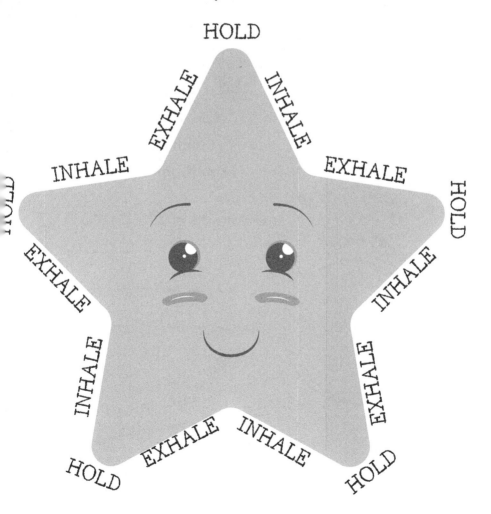

FEELINGS JOURNAL

today I feel...

DATE

today I am grateful for

I feel this because...

what I want to remember about today

- - - - - - - - -
- - - - - - - - -
- - - - - - - - -
- - - - - - - - -

feelings emoji

I'm proud of myself because

RANDOM THOUGHTS

Sometimes there are so many thoughts that go through our heads that we feel overwhelmed. Give yourself a few minutes and unleash your feelings and thoughts. It doesn't matter how random they are, just get them out.

it's okay to feel

your feelings

FEELINGS JOURNAL

DATE

today I feel...

today I am grateful for

I feel this because...

what I want to remember about today

- - - - - - - - - -

- - - - - - - - - -

- - - - - - - - - -

- - - - - - - - - -

feelings emoji

I'm proud of myself because

"Be yourself; everyone else is already taken."
~ Oscar Wilde

Be
Kind

FEELINGS JOURNAL

today I feel...

today I am grateful for

DATE

I feel this because...

what I want to remember about today

- - - - - - - - - - -

- - - - - - - - - - -

- - - - - - - - - - -

- - - - - - - - - - -

feelings emoji

I'm proud of myself because

"You are braver than you believe, stronger than you seem, and smarter than you think."
~ Christopher Robin, Winnie the Pooh

IT'S GONNA
BE OK

FEELINGS JOURNAL

DATE

today I feel...

today I am grateful for

I feel this because...

what I want to remember about today

feelings emoji

I'm proud of myself because

"Remember you're the one who can fill the world with sunshine."
~ Snow White, Snow White and the Seven Dwarfs

Trust Yourself

FEELINGS JOURNAL

DATE

today I feel...

today I am grateful for

I feel this because...

what I want to remember about today

- - - - - - - - - - - -

- - - - - - - - - - - -

- - - - - - - - - - - -

- - - - - - - - - - - -

feelings emoji

I'm proud of myself because

"Happiness is not something ready-made. It comes from your own actions."
~ Dalai Lama XIV

STAY
SAFE

FEELINGS JOURNAL

today I feel...

DATE

today I am grateful for

I feel this because...

what I want to remember about today

feelings emoji

- - - - - - - - - -

- - - - - - - - - -

- - - - - - - - - -

- - - - - - - - - -

I'm proud of myself because

"Being different isn't a bad thing. It means you're brave enough to be yourself."
~ Luna Lovegood, Harry Potter

Love
yourself

FEELINGS JOURNAL

DATE

today I feel...

today I am grateful for

I feel this because...

what I want to remember about today

- - - - - - - - - -

- - - - - - - - - -

- - - - - - - - - -

- - - - - - - - - -

feelings emoji

I'm proud of myself because

"If you have good thoughts they will shine out of your face like sunbeams and you will always look lovely."
~ Roald Dahl

keep going

FEELINGS JOURNAL

today I feel...

DATE

today I am grateful for

I feel this because...

what I want to remember about today

- - - - - - - -
- - - - - - - -
- - - - - - - -
- - - - - - - -

feelings emoji

I'm proud of myself because

"Never look down on anybody unless you're helping them up."
~ Jesse Jackson

Be
Better

FEELINGS JOURNAL

today I feel...

DATE

today I am grateful for

I feel this because...

what I want to remember about today

\- \- \- \- \- \- \- \-

\- \- \- \- \- \- \- \-

\- \- \- \- \- \- \- \-

\- \- \- \- \- \- \- \-

feelings emoji

I'm proud of myself because

"If you can dream it, you can do it."
~ Walt Disney

Let the
sunshine in

FEELINGS JOURNAL

DATE

today I feel...

today I am grateful for

I feel this because...

what I want to remember about today

- - - - - - - - - - - - - -

- - - - - - - - - - - - - -

- - - - - - - - - - - - - -

- - - - - - - - - - - - - -

feelings emoji

I'm proud of myself because

"It's not what happens to you, but how you react
to it that matters."
~ Epictetus

Think
Positive

FEELINGS JOURNAL

today I feel...

DATE

today I am grateful for

I feel this because...

what I want to remember about today

feelings emoji

I'm proud of myself because

"Feelings are much like waves, we can't stop them from coming, but we can choose which one to surf."
~ Jonathan Martensson

it's okay to feel

your feelings

"The pain of a hard goodbye is the heart's tribute to the privilege to love"

~ Beth Moore

GOODBYE LETTER

To: _____

I am saying goodbye because: _____

_____

Saying goodbye makes me feel: _____

_____

I remember a time when we: _____

_____

You taught me to: _____

_____

Something I want you to know is: _____

_____

I will always remember: _____

_____

♡ ♡ ♡   From: _____

"There's a great big beautiful tomorrow shining at the end of every day."

~ Walt Disney

 # CONCLUSION

Here we are at the end of this incredible journey. Congratulations, you've made it! You must be so proud of yourself!

Before parting our ways remember that there are times in life when unexpected things occur, but it's up to us how we face them. It is important to know how to manage our feelings and thoughts to be able to cope better when such situations appear. You did exactly that. I hope going through these pages helped you better understand yourself. You are so brave! You are an inspiration to everyone around you.

Even if you completed this quest, there may be moments when you won't fully understand your emotions. Sometimes it's ok not to be ok. It's ok to feel whatever you are feeling. Revisit this journal whenever you think you need it.

You've come a long way. Just be kind to yourself!

~ With love, Hope

thank you

This is Hope from <u>Publish To Inspire</u>. I just want to thank you for going through this journal with me. I really hope it was helpful to you. Remember, all storms will eventually pass, and the sun will shine brighter. You are a strong and incredible person!!

Publish To Inspire is a small family company, so your feedback is very important to us. Please let us know how you like our book at: <u>contact@publishtoinspire.com</u>.

If you are interested in some extra activities we have a surprise for you. Visit our website and get some free goodies.
<u>https://publish-to-inspire.my.canva.site/</u>

Made in the USA
Las Vegas, NV
23 December 2024

15150841R00056